STICKMEN'S GUIDE TO OCEANS

IN LAYERS

Thanks to the creative team:
Senior Editor: Alice Peebles
Fact checking: Kate Mitchell
Design: www.collaborate.agency

Hungry Tomato™
A division of Lerner Publishing Group, Inc.
241 First Avenue North
Minneapolis, MN 55401 USA

For reading levels and more information, look up this title at www.lernerbooks.com.

Main body text set in Avenir Next Medium 9.5/12. Typeface provided by Linotype AG.

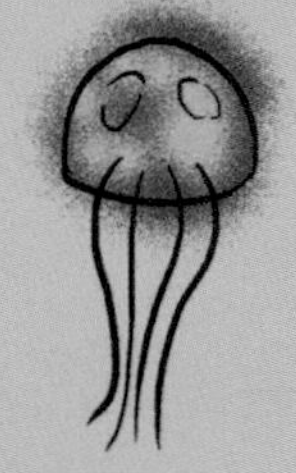

Library of Congress Cataloging-in-Publication Data

The Cataloging-in-Publication Data for *Stickmen's Guide to Oceans in Layers* is on file at the Library of Congress.
ISBN 978-1-5124-0619-1 (lib. bdg.)
ISBN 978-1-5124-1180-5 (pbk.)
ISBN 978-1-5124-0933-8 (EB pdf)

Manufactured in the United States of America
1 - VP - 7/15/16

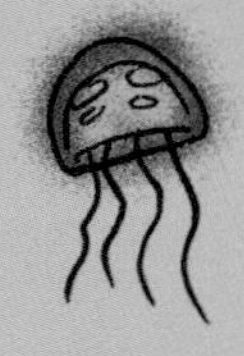

STICKMEN'S GUIDE TO OCEANS IN LAYERS

by Catherine Chambers
Illustrated by John Paul de Quay

Contents

Oceans

Earth's oceans are vast connected bowls of dark basalt rock. Oceans cover 72 percent of the world and provide 70 percent of our oxygen. These oceans filled with water that was created by gaseous clouds billowing over prehistoric Earth. Ocean crusts began to form less than 200 million years ago and now hold water at an average depth of 13,000 feet (4,000 meters).

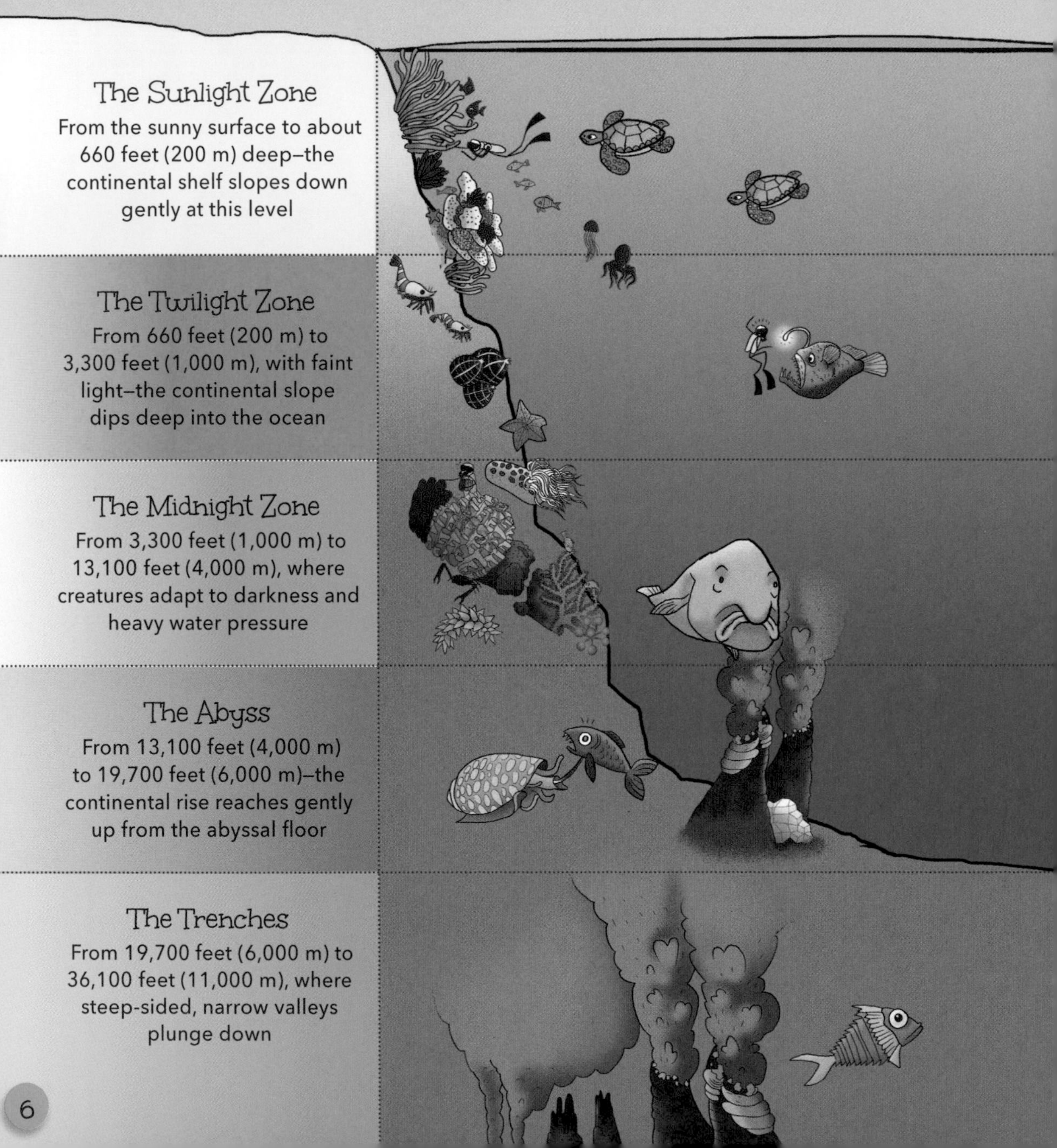

ORCA

The Sunlight Zone

In our oceans' top layer, the sun's light flickers and filters through waters that teem with life. The sun's rays grow dimmer further down the layer. But these murkier depths are still full of brightly colored plants and creatures.

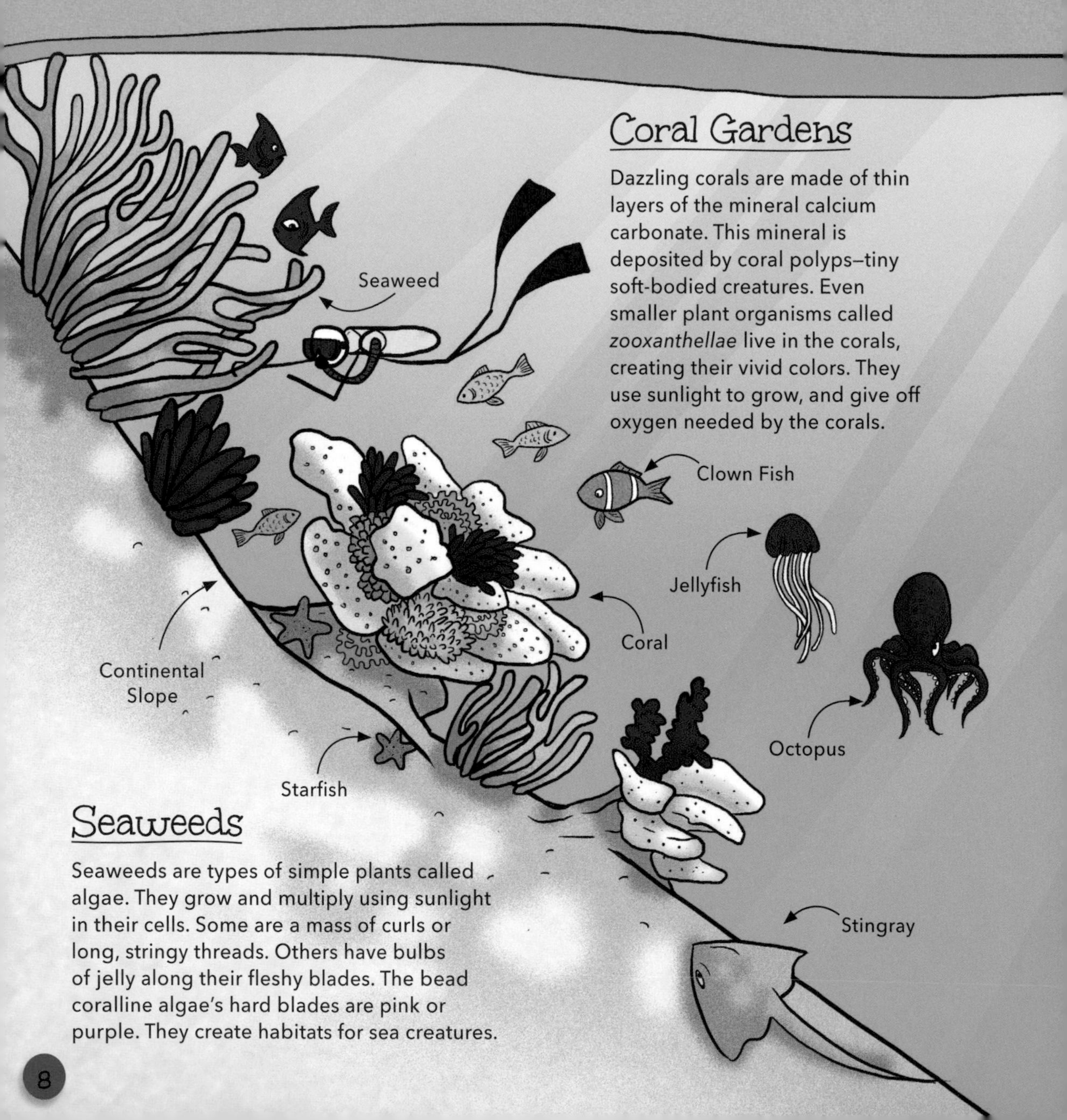

Coral Gardens

Dazzling corals are made of thin layers of the mineral calcium carbonate. This mineral is deposited by coral polyps—tiny soft-bodied creatures. Even smaller plant organisms called *zooxanthellae* live in the corals, creating their vivid colors. They use sunlight to grow, and give off oxygen needed by the corals.

Seaweeds

Seaweeds are types of simple plants called algae. They grow and multiply using sunlight in their cells. Some are a mass of curls or long, stringy threads. Others have bulbs of jelly along their fleshy blades. The bead coralline algae's hard blades are pink or purple. They create habitats for sea creatures.

Microscopic Life

Swarms of microscopic phytoplankton (plants) and zooplankton (animals) begin our oceans' food chain. A species called *eukaryotic phytoplankton* helps to regulate climate by absorbing carbon gases.

Munch, Munch

This huge and rare sea mammal is a right whale. It is 50 feet (15 m) long and weighs the same as three heavy trucks. Yet this massive creature feeds on tiny shrimp-like copepods, swallowing up to 2,600 pounds (1,180 kilograms) of them each day. It filters the copepods through two rows of comb-like plates called *baleen*.

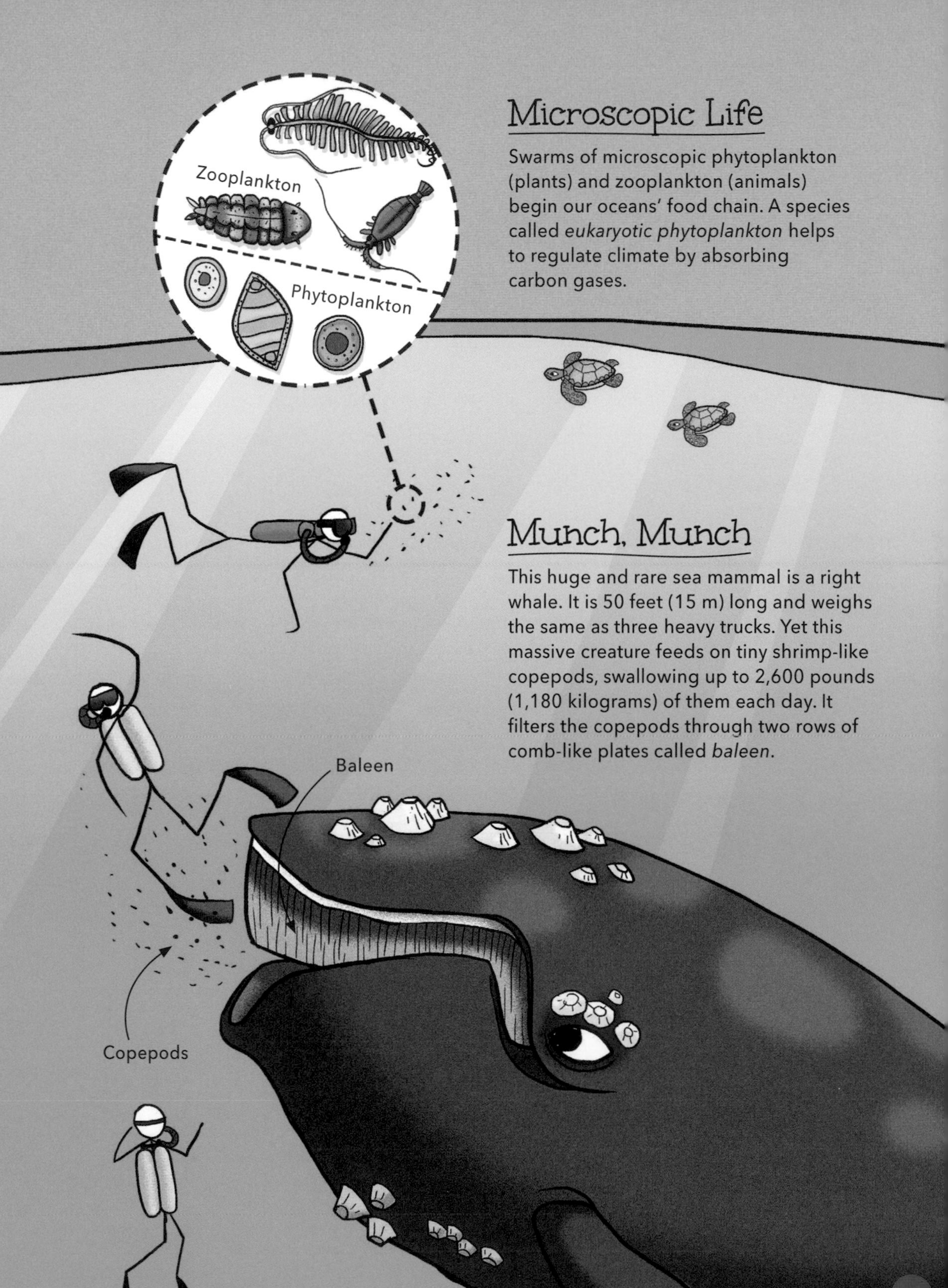

Superhighway

The sunlight zone is a well-used highway for humans. We design gigantic vessels to transport vast quantities of goods across it, from port to distant port. We fish in it, exploit its riches, and extract oil from its depths.

Let's Go Fishing

Nearly 90 percent of marine life is found in the sunlight zone. This includes vast numbers of fish caught on the world's 4 million fishing vessels. These range from tiny rowing boats to massive trawlers that can freeze fish on board. Trawlers sail on the sunlight zone but often catch fish way below it.

Trash Islands

Islands of litter, which has been dumped or washed into the sea, float on the oceans. Plastic bags gather in a massive tangle, dragging in fishing gear, bottles, boat parts, and other debris. They choke marine life and darken the waters below. As the plastics break down, they release tiny particles and toxic chemicals that enter the food chain.

On the Ocean Wave

The first ocean-going cargo ships were galleys, powered by rowing. They began to sail from the Mediterranean Sea into the Atlantic Ocean in about 1280BCE. Goods could then reach northern Europe more easily than across mountainous lands. Ships got larger, and allowed for fishing in open waters.

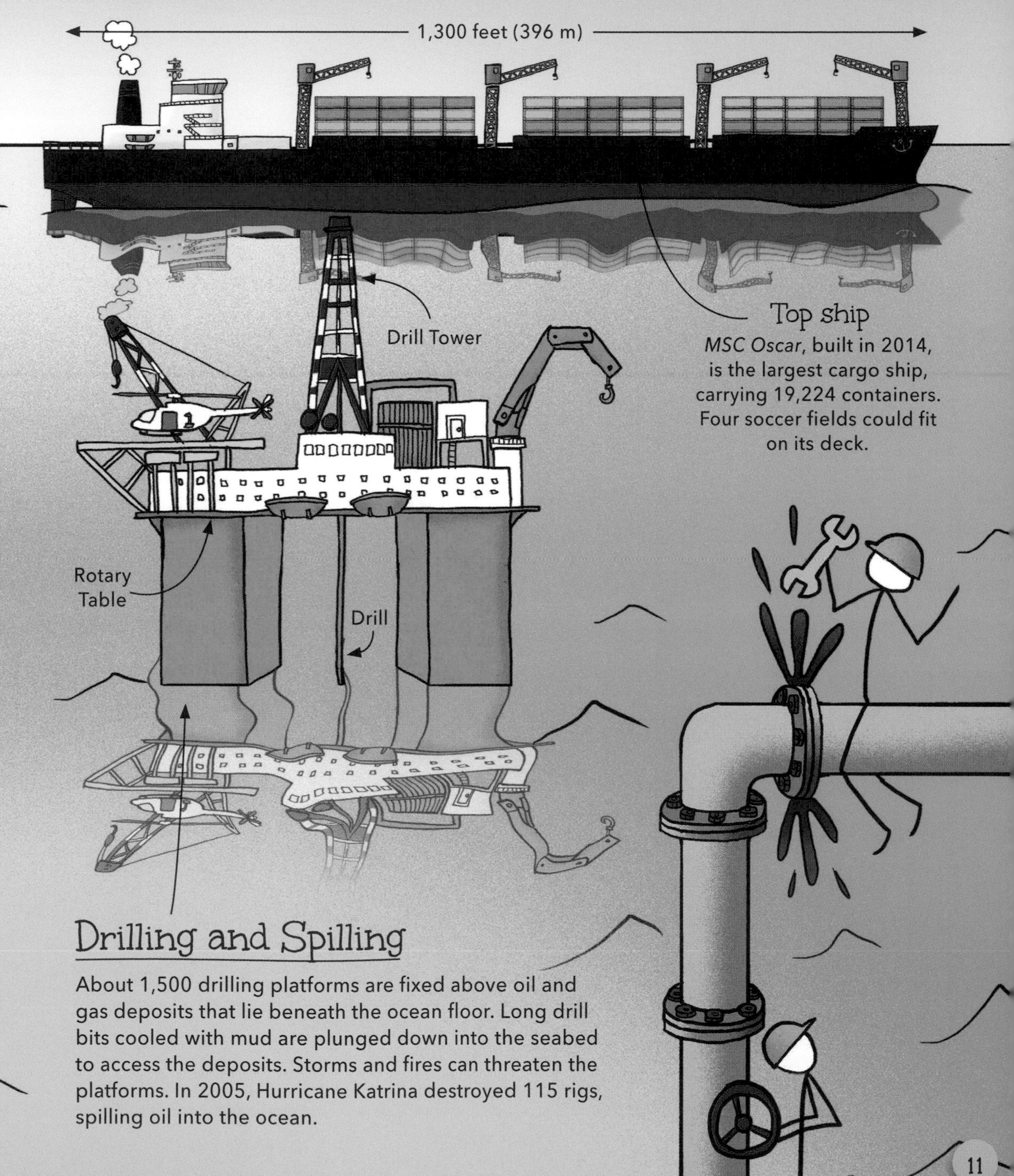

Top ship

MSC Oscar, built in 2014, is the largest cargo ship, carrying 19,224 containers. Four soccer fields could fit on its deck.

Drilling and Spilling

About 1,500 drilling platforms are fixed above oil and gas deposits that lie beneath the ocean floor. Long drill bits cooled with mud are plunged down into the seabed to access the deposits. Storms and fires can threaten the platforms. In 2005, Hurricane Katrina destroyed 115 rigs, spilling oil into the ocean.

The Twilight Zone

The twilight zone's waters are cold and murky. Only a faint light reaches this ocean layer during the day, and everything appears a dark, indigo blue. Water pressure is high and there is little oxygen. Yet there is still plenty of life.

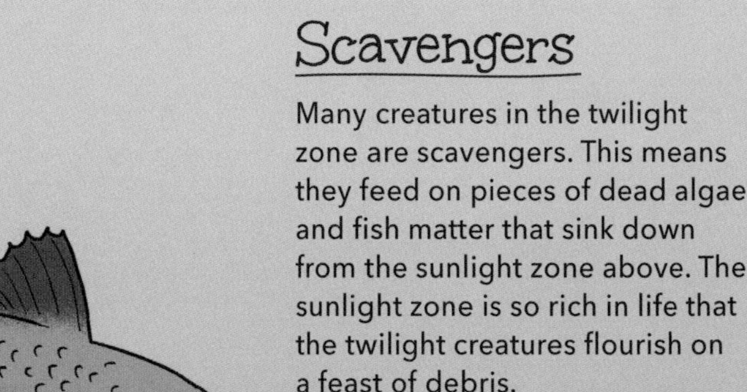

Scavengers

Many creatures in the twilight zone are scavengers. This means they feed on pieces of dead algae and fish matter that sink down from the sunlight zone above. The sunlight zone is so rich in life that the twilight creatures flourish on a feast of debris.

Continental Slope

Here, the seabed angles steeply down from the continental shelf. This is called the continental slope. Sea creatures cling to or crawl along it.

Continental Slope

Armed Nylon Shrimp

Purple Sea Urchin

Cushion Sea Star

Shells and Spines

Crustaceans, such as crab and shrimp species, have hard, flexible exoskeletons protecting their bodies. Some scuttle along the seabed, chasing their prey. Others filter plankton and bacteria from the water. The spiny purple sea urchin uses its tentacle suckers, or tube feet, to breathe, move, and feed.

Squid Hunt

Huge sperm whales dive down over 3,000 feet (900 m) through this layer to hunt for giant squid below. These whales find their prey through echolocation, making loud clicking sounds that hit the squid and bounce back to them. This tells the whales where the giant squid are.

Whale sends and receives sound

Attaching equipment to monitor whale sound

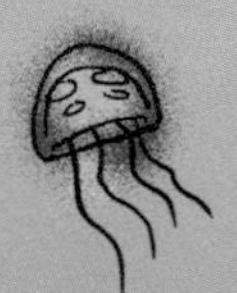

Glowing Bacteria

Spark in the Dark

Many creatures in these dark depths make their own blue-green or red bioluminescent light to attract prey or a mate. The female anglerfish extends the spine of her back fin above her head, like a fishing rod. At the end, a light made of glowing bacteria lures her prey.

Carbon Sinks

Scientists lower instruments to measure the amount of carbon dioxide in the oceans. Too much carbon in the atmosphere contributes to climate change. But some ocean organisms absorb carbon dioxide, removing it from the atmosphere. The microscopic copepod excretes its carbon-trapped waste that sinks to the oceans' depths.

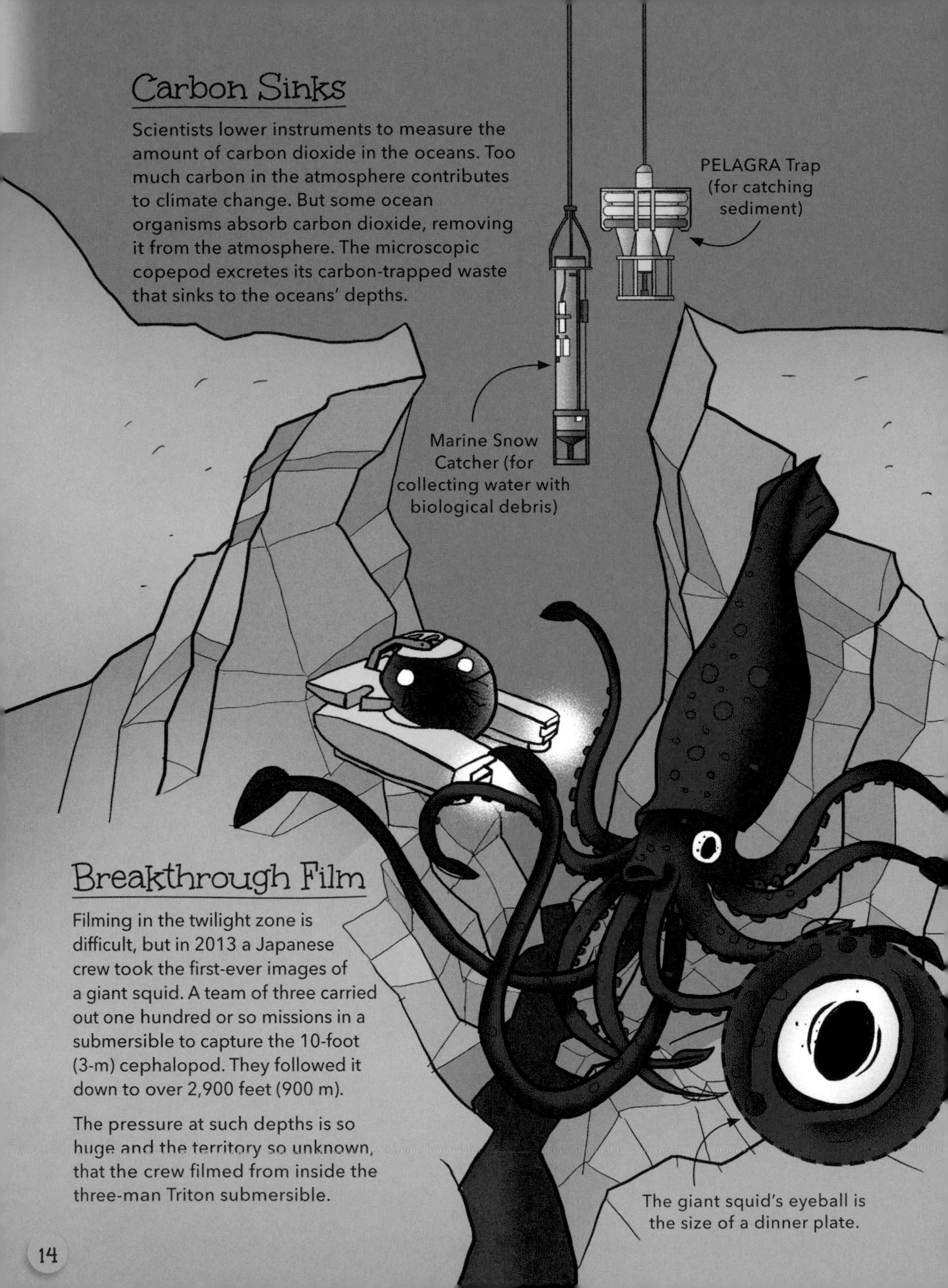

PELAGRA Trap (for catching sediment)

Marine Snow Catcher (for collecting water with biological debris)

Breakthrough Film

Filming in the twilight zone is difficult, but in 2013 a Japanese crew took the first-ever images of a giant squid. A team of three carried out one hundred or so missions in a submersible to capture the 10-foot (3-m) cephalopod. They followed it down to over 2,900 feet (900 m).

The pressure at such depths is so huge and the territory so unknown, that the crew filmed from inside the three-man Triton submersible.

The giant squid's eyeball is the size of a dinner plate.

Exploring the Seabed

The twilight zone is a very exciting place for oceanography, the study of our oceans. Scientists observe sea creatures, from microorganisms to the giant squid, and watch for signs of climate change on Earth.

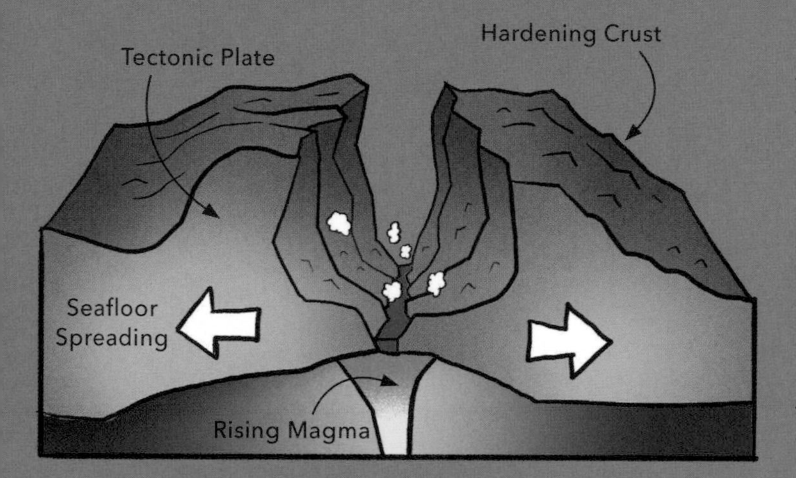

Mid-ocean Ridge

From parts of the twilight zone to deep on the ocean floor, ridges of crusty rock lie on the edges of two great slabs of seabed. These are tectonic plates that spread apart, allowing hot magma beneath to rise. Here the water cools the magma to form crusty toppings. This mid-ocean ridge was not explored until 1973.

The First Explorers

In 1934, scientist William Beebe joined engineer Otis Barton in Barton's bathysphere (right). The two Americans were the first to reach the twilight zone.

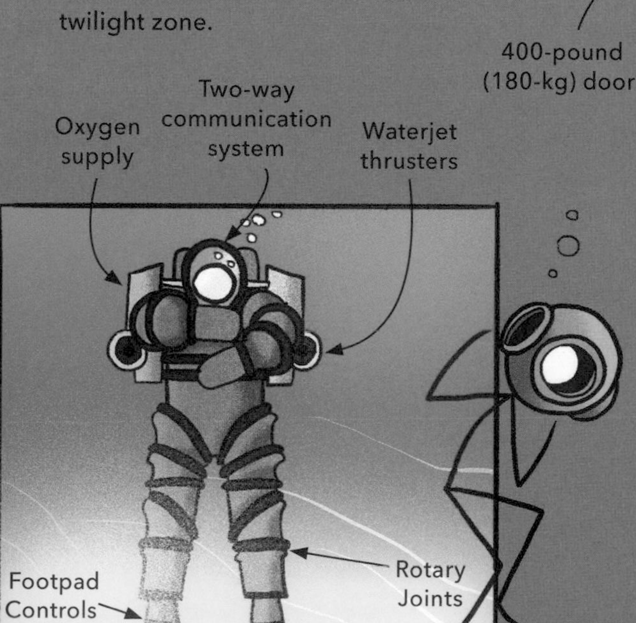

Deep-sea Diving

Divers need very strong suits to withstand high pressure at this level. The Exosuit (left) allows divers to plunge 1,000 feet (300 m) below the surface. It can withstand high pressure even at its weakest joints. An operator at the surface monitors conditions in the Exosuit through inbuilt links and can maneuver the suit, and the diver, away from danger.

The Midnight Zone

The chilly midnight zone occupies up to 90 percent of our oceans. The only natural light here in the deep is made by bioluminescent life-forms. Many creatures are black or red to hide in the near total darkness, and some have very large eyes—or no eyes at all.

Walking Cucumbers

Sea cucumbers are echinoderms, which means they have spiny skins. They feed on debris floating in the sea or buried in the sand. Sea cucumbers move around on rows of tube feet with suckers. Some eject a tangle of threads, toxins, or even their own internal organs to put off predators.

Cuttlefish

Blobfish

Sea Cucumbers

Jelly or Fish?

The jelly-like blobfish floats just above the ocean floor in Australia's deep waters. It has almost no muscle and cannot swim. It feeds by keeping its mouth open to take in small pieces of food debris. No one has yet seen a blobfish that is more than 12 inches (30.48 centimeters) long.

Shiny Shark

The cookie-cutter shark is a fast swimmer that can descend to 12,000 feet (3,700 m). It shines with a bright green bioluminescence made by photophore organs that emit light. This small shark grows 20 inches (50 cm) long at most, but its razor-sharp teeth bite chunks out of much larger prey, leaving cookie-cutter marks on their flesh.

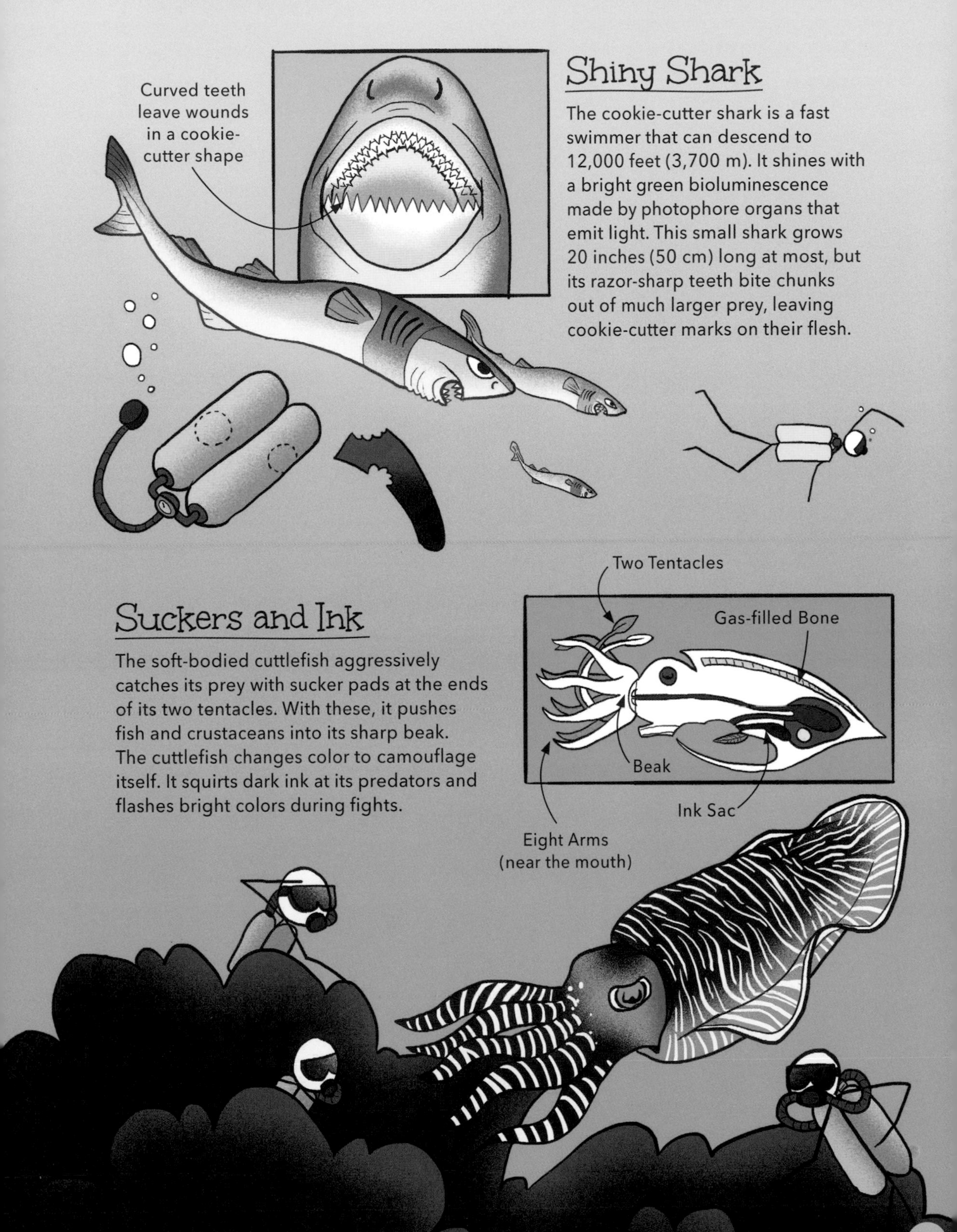

Suckers and Ink

The soft-bodied cuttlefish aggressively catches its prey with sucker pads at the ends of its two tentacles. With these, it pushes fish and crustaceans into its sharp beak. The cuttlefish changes color to camouflage itself. It squirts dark ink at its predators and flashes bright colors during fights.

Deep-sea Discoveries

The life-forms of the midnight zone are continually under investigation. Scientists lower special traps that delicately lift up tender creatures without damaging them. They also observe microscopic organisms that feed and breathe by chemosynthesis, absorbing chemicals from the water.

Softly, Softly

Sponges are soft creatures made of hundreds of special cells that help them survive. They have no internal organs. Some are scavengers, while others are predators. Once, humans harvested them to use in the bath. Now, researchers study some of the 8,500 or so species to discover more about evolution.

Sponges stick to rock or move 0.04 inch (1 millimeter) per day.

Sponge Medicine

Scientists study deep-sea sponges to find new treatments and cures for diseases. Some sponges contain chemicals that are being developed into medicines to fight infections. One deep-water species, *Discodermia dissoluta*, is of special interest. It may have properties that reduce some cancerous tumors.

Cells for Research (growing in a petri dish)

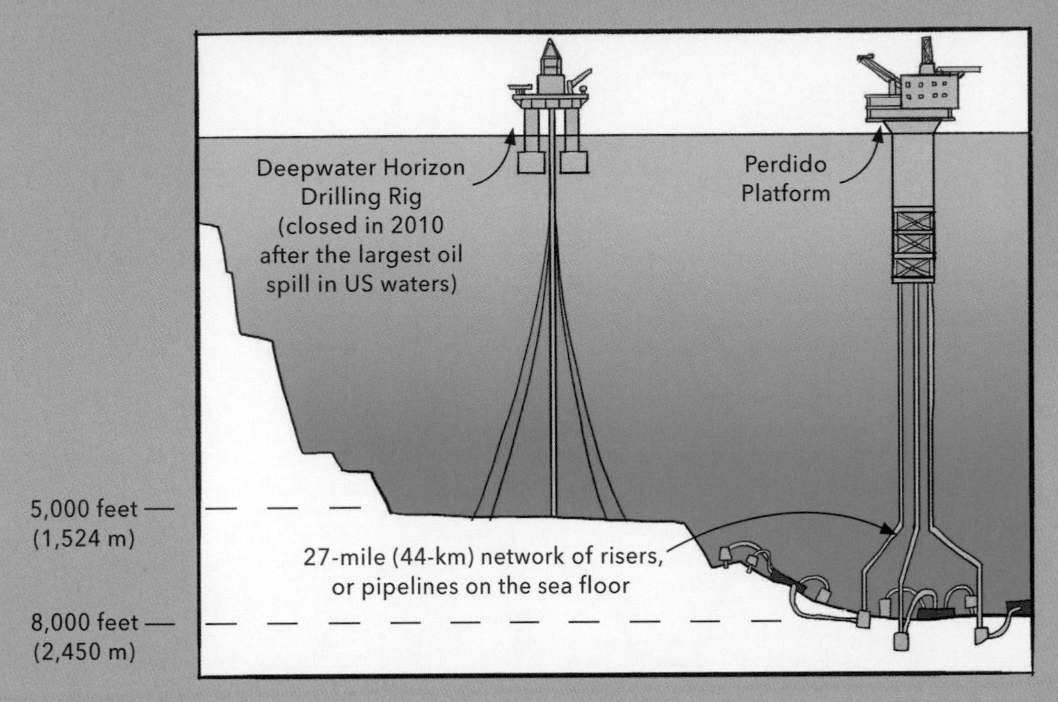

Deepest Well

In the Gulf of Mexico, the Perdido platform sits in 8,000 feet (2,450 m) of water above the deepest oil and gas well, which was drilled 1.9 miles (3 km) into the seabed. Perdido means "lost" in Spanish!

Photo Shoot

Remote-control cameras that withstand enormous water pressure capture images of coral gardens. Corals are important habitats for other life-forms and can act as indicators of climate change. More than 4,800 coral species have been found so far, more than half in the deep sea. Some are as tiny as a small seed, while others grow as tall a house.

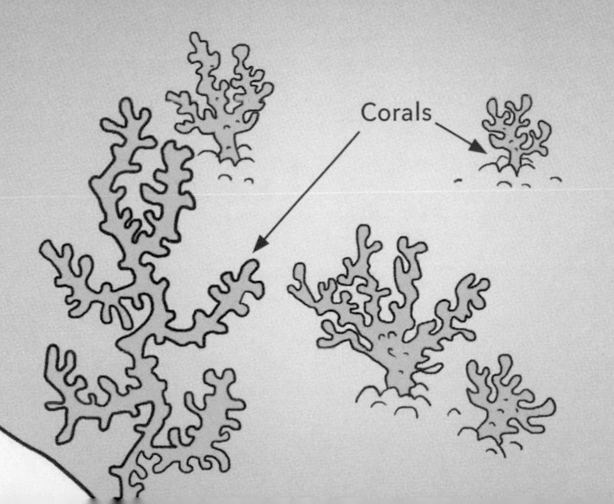

Strong
Camera Cage

Temperatures:
122-752°F
(50-400°C)

Smoking Chimneys

Hydrothermal vents form on the ocean floor above hot moving magma. Cracks in the floor allow seawater to seep in. This water is heated by the magma and bubbles up again. The boiling water brings with it dissolved rock minerals that harden into a crust, which builds up into chimneys.

Hydrothermal Plume
(containing oxygen, sulfur, or acids)

Hydrothermal Vent

Polychaete Worm
(with bristly body segments)

Chilled Out

In the Gulf of Mexico and away from the warm vents, a species of polychaete worm, or bristle worm, lives in chilly methane ice-burrows.

The Black Abyss

The abyss is mostly a pitch black, icy zone, but life still exists here. And where the ocean floor lies close to inner Earth's hot magma, hydrothermal vents occur. Discovered only in 1977, these vents teem with creatures that, amazingly, survive the most hostile conditions.

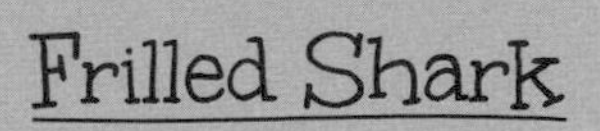

Frilled Shark

The frilled shark is rarely seen but we know that its eel-like body is about 6 feet (1.8 m) long. It catches prey half its size with three hundred needle-like teeth. It is named after the six frill-like gill slits at the sides of its head through which it takes in oxygen.

Frilly Gill Slits

Dead Vent

Stalked Jellyfish

See-through Creatures

Translucent stalked jellyfish live mostly near the shore, but new species have been found clustering around dead hydrothermal vents. Stalked jellyfish move very slowly, just shifting their position slightly. They are hard to spot as their color is adapted to blend in with their habitat.

Giant Tube Worms

These bright red translucent creatures live around the chimneys of warm hydrothermal vents. They have no eyes, mouth, or stomach. Tube worms use energy passed down by bacteria that live on them. The bacteria take in the chemical hydrogen sulphide from the vent, and this keeps the tube worms alive. In turn the bacteria live on the tube worm's blood.

A tube worm's blood gives it a red color.

Secrets of the Abyss

To explore the abyss, scientists use state-of-the-art technology to map its hidden crevices, monitor important global currents, and look for new marine species. The discovery of hydrothermal vents (see pages 20–21) also revealed deposits of precious minerals, such as cobalt and gold.

GPS Satellite

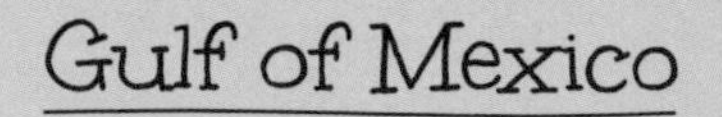

Gulf of Mexico

This is a hotspot for scientific research because of its rich deep-sea habitats, from coral mounds and glades to salty pools and expanses of mud.

Hydrophone (for measuring sound)

Echo Sounder (bouncing beams)

Mapping the Floor

Oceanographers survey the seabed first by using the Global Positioning System (GPS) and official coast guard coordinates to record the position. Echo-sounding equipment profiles the undulating ocean floor. Digital hydrophones convert sounds into electrical energy, which can be measured at the surface.

Reflected Sound Waves

Boom Arms
(for grabbers and
instruments)

Underwater Robotics

Robotic submarines controlled from the surface explore and record conditions in the abyss. Some grab samples to bring up for research. Others use fiber-optic technology to capture 3D videos and still images. Microphones pick up such sounds as whale song and volcanic eruptions on the ocean floor.

Currents

Oceanographers observe deep-sea currents closely, as their movement, temperature, and salt content give clues to climate change. The Antarctic Circumpolar Current begins with freezing, dense salty water sinking, which starts movement in this zone. It meets and mixes with warmer water and flows to other regions.

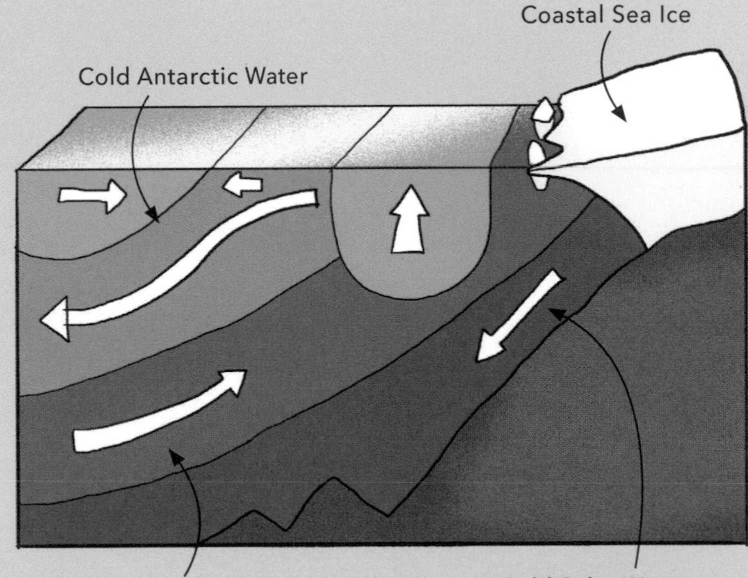

Useful Venom

Scientists are looking ever deeper for new species that may have unexpected benefits for humans. The cone snail's lethal venom contains a wide range of chemicals that are being developed into medicines, including painkillers. The creature's powerful poison is unleashed through a long tongue called a *proboscis*.

The Ocean's Trenches

Ocean floors rise and fall with Earth's highest mountains and deepest valleys, or trenches. Trenches can plunge down 5–6 miles (8–10 km) and are slightly warmer than the abyss above. Their habitats are rocky, though softer sediment lies at some bases.

No Buoyancy Swim Bladder

Translucent Fish

V-shaped Trench

Trench Formation

Most trenches are V-shaped and are formed where one oceanic plate slides beneath another. Volcanic islands often lie around a trench's rim.

Under Pressure

Water pressure in the trenches is extreme. The gas-filled swim bladder that gives a fish buoyancy is not present in many deep-sea species. Instead these fish produce heavy concentrations of a chemical that helps the body's cells withstand pressure.

Volcanoes

Strings of underwater volcanoes run for miles on the deep-ocean floor. In 2011, sonar images captured the Tonga Trench as it swallowed giant volcanoes into its depths. This trench is an active fault line that runs north of New Zealand toward the small islands of Tonga and Samoa in the South Pacific Ocean. It reaches 6.7 miles (10.9 km) down at its deepest.

Trench Fish

Delicate, translucent snailfish survive the depths of the trenches. In 2014, a new species was discovered 5 miles (8 km) down in the Mariana Trench. This snailfish's head is dog-shaped and its fins are very broad. Scientists believe the sensors that cover the fins detect prey in the soft mud.

Broad fins on a snailfish

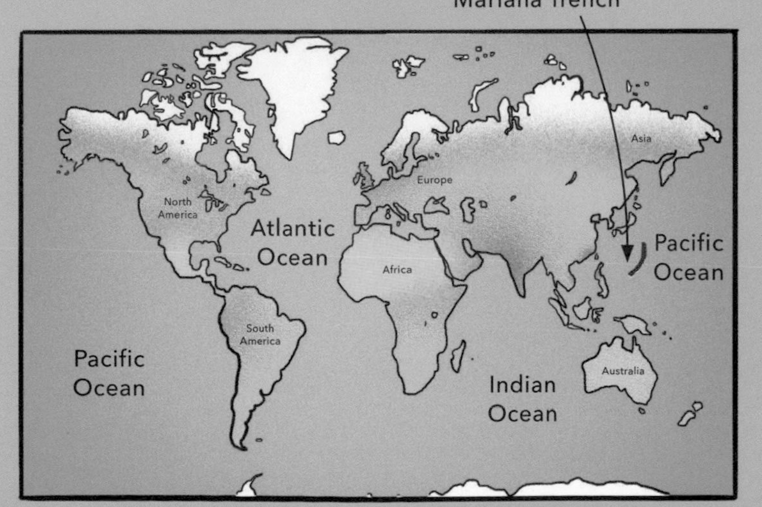

Deep, Deeper . . .

The Mariana Trench is the deepest in our oceans. Its lowest point is the Challenger Deep, 6.83 miles (10.99 km) down. In 2005, scientists examined samples from its soil. They were surprised to find the single-celled foraminifera organism, which has a soft shell, living so deep down. It is normally found in the layers above.

Taking the Plunge

The trenches are an exciting wilderness for scientists but conditions there are tough. Equipment has to withstand water pressure weighing almost the same as fifty jumbo jets. Research has to be carefully managed so that habitats are not destroyed.

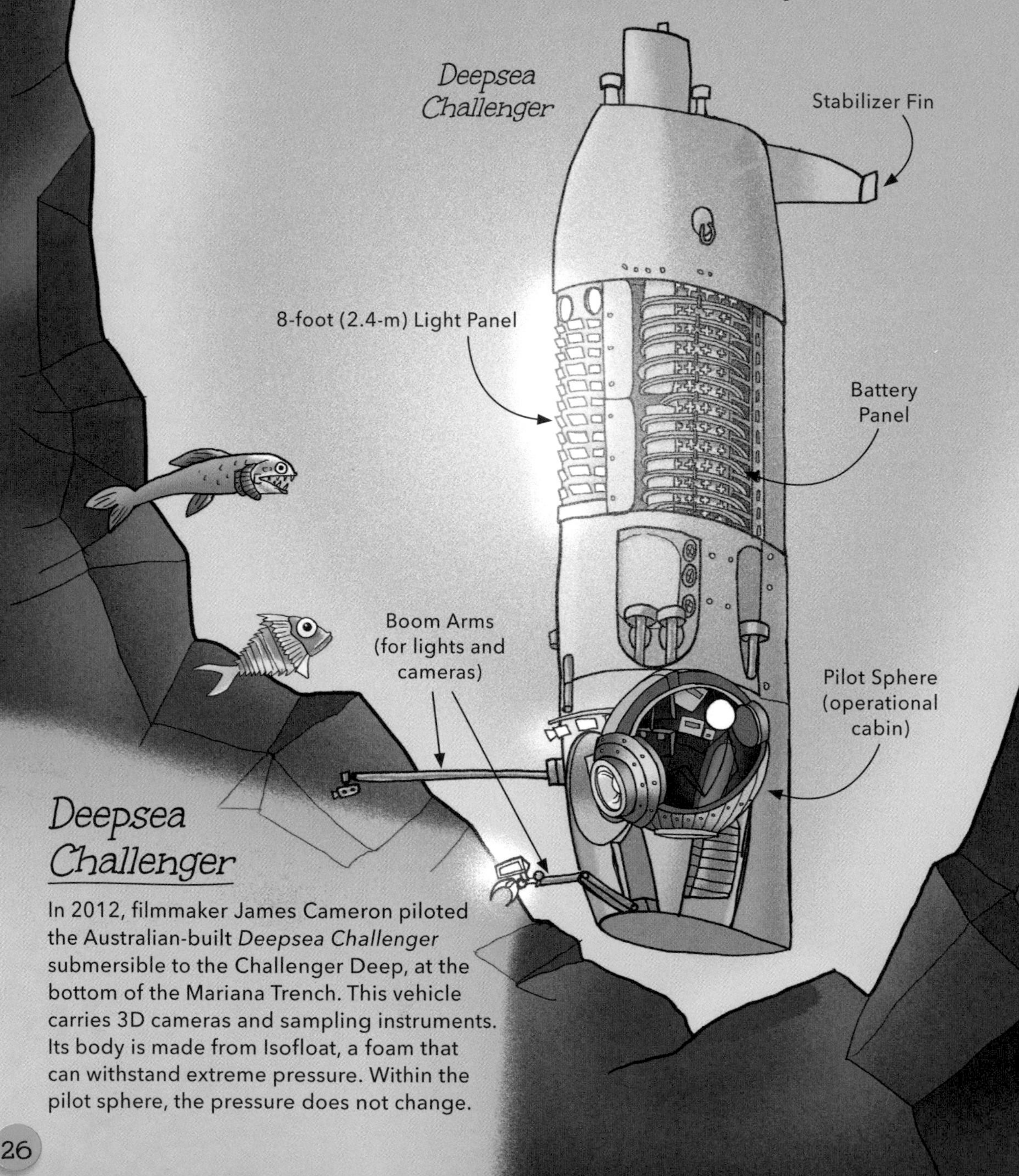

Deepsea Challenger

In 2012, filmmaker James Cameron piloted the Australian-built *Deepsea Challenger* submersible to the Challenger Deep, at the bottom of the Mariana Trench. This vehicle carries 3D cameras and sampling instruments. Its body is made from Isofloat, a foam that can withstand extreme pressure. Within the pilot sphere, the pressure does not change.

Mapping the Trenches

Echo sounding maps the shape of our deeply plunging seabed. Echo sounders work by reflecting sound waves off the bottom. The waves' lengths show the rise and fall of the ocean floor. Echo sounding was first used in 1920 by German physicist Alexander Behm.

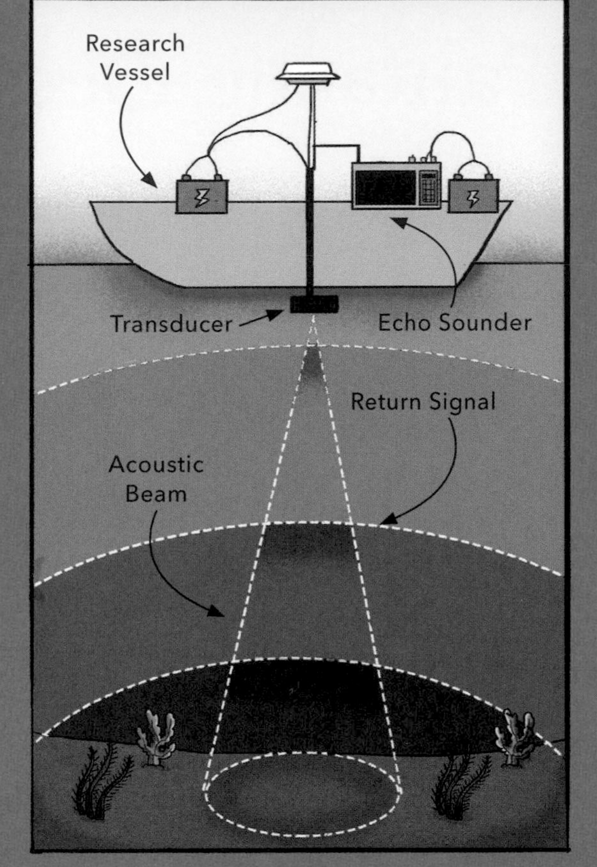

ORCA Camera

Deep down this "Eye-in-the-Sea" illuminates the image in front of it using powerful red lights that most creatures in this zone cannot see.

Tracking Earthquakes

The trenches help us to find ways of monitoring earth tremors. Hydrophone instruments (right) are lowered into the trench. These measure the pressure from any movement in the trench floor. The hydrophones' transponders (the yellow spheres) convert the movements into electrical signals that are analyzed at the surface.

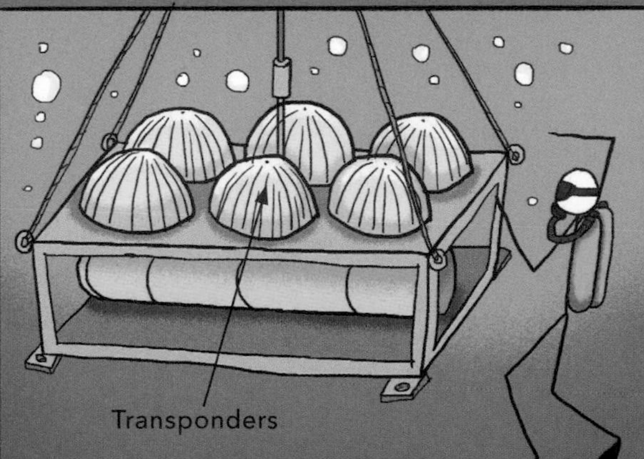

Fantastic Ocean Facts

Great Pacific Garbage Patches

Plastic litter "islands" cover an amazing 1,931 square miles (5,000 square kilometers) of the Pacific Ocean. The "islands"are not solid, consisting mostly of small plastic pieces and microplastics. The two largest are the Western Pacific Garbage Patch toward Japan, and the Eastern Pacific Garbage Patch toward California.

Toxic Algae

Close to forty out of four thousand species of microscopic phytoplankton algae are highly poisonous, killing millions of fish and shellfish! In recent decades they have grown into huge floating red blankets, called blooms. In 2015, a giant floating bloom was seen stretching from the central California coast all the way up to Washington in the United States.

Dense Underwater Forests

Giant kelp is a variety of seaweed that forms thick underwater forests. This towering brown algae can grow up to 18 inches (46 cm) each day, to a height of 175 feet (53 m). Air bladders help its dense canopy to float on top of the water, sheltering thousands of fish and shellfish species, and even seals and whales.

Colossal Coral Reef

Off the east coast of Australia lies the largest living structure on Earth, the Great Barrier Reef. This mass of six hundred hard and soft corals stretches 1,429 miles (2,300 km) and covers 132,974 square miles (344,400 sq km). Its different habitats provide perfect conditions for 1,625 varieties of fish, 3,000 kinds of molluscs,133 shark species, and many more.

Deep-sea Archaeology

Digging for history can take place on the ocean floor! Here, marine archaeologists find sunken artefacts—and occasionally, treasure. In 350BCE, a heavily-laden ancient Greek cargo ship sank in the Aegean Sea. About 2,350 years later, a robot detected its cargo of elegant jars, or *amphorae*, containing olive oil!

Shark Shocks

Sharks were around 200 million years before dinosaurs! So they've had plenty of time to evolve into more than 465 species. They range in size from the tiny spined pygmy shark at 7 inches (18 cm), to the 50-foot (15-m) whale shark. They use their nostrils solely for smelling, which is why some species can detect one part of blood in a million parts of water!

Super Starfish

Starfish, or sea stars, have five arms each but they don't worry if they lose a few, as they just grow more! Each arm has an eye at the end of it, which can detect light, dark, and basic shapes. Starfish have no brains or blood. They can feel, though, because they have a nervous system that spreads through their arms.

Tallest Mountain

The highest mountain on land is Mt. Everest, at 29,035 feet (8,850 m). But the tallest mountain from the base to the summit is Mauna Kea, which rises 33,465 feet (10,200 m) from the bottom of the Pacific Ocean. On land, its peak rises to 13,796 feet (4,205 m). Mauna Kea is an inactive volcano and formed more than one million years ago.

The Future...

We know less about vast areas of our oceans than about any other habitat on Earth. We do know that they hold precious resources and treatments for diseases. But our oceans need care.

Climate Change

Our climate has warmed fast over the last two hundred years. Most scientists believe that burning fossil fuels has caused this by releasing too much carbon dioxide into the air. Carbon gases absorb warmth, which cannot escape into the upper atmosphere. Instead, it is reflected back onto Earth. The rise in temperature affects ocean layers.

Rising Seas

A warming climate makes sea levels rise by melting ice at the poles. Higher sea levels may even threaten to drown small low-lying islands and even towns and cities along continental coastlines. A warmer climate also increases the strength of cyclones and the damaging effects of waves.

Overfishing

Fishing fleets trawl with huge nets in the deep ocean. They have reduced fish stocks, threatened species, and destroyed some deep-sea habitats. The biggest trawler ever built was *Atlantic Dawn*, at 472 feet (144 m) long. It located huge shoals of fish using sonar technology and could process and freeze 400 tons (363 tonnes) of fish every twenty-four hours.

Ocean Clean-up

Oil spills and plastic bag islands pollute our oceans. Climate change has led to vast blankets of toxic algae floating on the surface. But new technology is helping to clean up the seas. The Ocean Cleanup Array is a 6,500-foot (2,000-m) flexible ring designed to enclose plastic waste so it can be removed. It is hoped that by 2021 it will have cleaned up half the Great Pacific Garbage Patch between Hawaii and California.